Secret History

ALSO BY DAVID BARBER

The Spirit Level

Wonder Cabinet

Secret History

POEMS

DAVID BARBER

TriQuarterly Books/Northwestern University Press
Evanston, Illinois

TriQuarterly Books
Northwestern University Press
www.nupress.northwestern.edu

Printed in the United States of America

10   9   8   7   6   5   4   3   2   1

Library of Congress Cataloging-in-Publication Data
Names: Barber, David, 1960– author.
Title: Secret history : poems / David Barber.
Description: Evanston, Illinois : TriQuarterly Books/Northwestern University
    Press, 2020.
Identifiers: LCCN 2019027215 | ISBN 9780810141223 (trade paperback) |
    ISBN 9780810141261 (ebook)
Subjects: LCGFT: Poetry.
Classification: LCC PS3552.A59194 A6 2020 | DDC 811/.54—dc23
LC record available at https://lccn.loc.gov/2019027215

For Jane & Sam

Blue skies

Every force evolves a form.
—MOTHER ANN LEE

One never knows, do one?
—FATS WALLER

CONTENTS

Secret History

ARIA

What if it were possible to vanquish
All this shame with a wash of varnish
Instead of wishing the stain would vanish?

What if you gave it a glossy finish?
What if there were a way to burnish
All this foolishness, all the anguish?

What if you gave yourself leave to ravish
All these ravages with famished relish?
What if this were your way to flourish?

What if the self you love to punish—
Knavish, peevish, wolfish, sheepish—
Were all slicked up in something lavish?

Why so squeamish? Why make a fetish
Out of everything you must relinquish?
Why not embellish what you can't abolish?

What would be left if you couldn't brandish
All the slavishness you've failed to banish?
What would you be without this gibberish?

What if the true worth of the varnish
Were to replenish your resolve to vanquish
Every vain wish before you vanish?

PRAXITELEAN

The body of a god,
A god in human form,
The form named for a man,
The name a shorthand for
A body like a god's.

A body hewn from stone,
The stone so finely formed
The name's a paradigm
For a chiseled figure
In flesh and blood.

The body an icon
In kind, man the measure
Of god-given proportion,
And no one so agog
As the son who sprang from

The state champion's loins,
The body of a man
At home in the gym,
The body his shrine,
A body to die for.

The body of a god,
A golden boy on
The rings and bars, a name
In stone all too human
No longer, true to form.

FRANKLIN ARITHMETIC

Springfield, Mass. 1832

How many hands have a boy and a clock?

Take E away from the word HOPE, and how many letters would be left? And what would it be then?

A man had seven children; two of them were killed by the fall of a tree; how many had he left?

Four rivers ran through the Garden of Eden, and one through Babylon; how many more ran through Eden than Babylon?

George Washington was 6 feet high; his shadow at noon was in summer 2 feet long; how long then is the shadow of a steeple 150 feet high?

A boy played three days in a week; how much did he work?

A bird can fly 60 miles an hour; how far in 10 hours? To fly from Providence to Jerusalem, how long?

In eighteen hundred and thirty we had in the United States 200 thousand slaves, but in seventeen hundred ninety, only 100 thousand; by how much did the slave trade go up?

Adonibezek said, "3 score and 10 kings, having their thumbs and great toes cut off, gather their meat under my table"; how many thumbs and toes did Adonibezek cut off?

The Nile is 20 hundred, and the Ohio 10 hundred miles long; the Ohio is what part of the Nile?

A boy was sick, in February, a fortnight; how many mornings was he up and about?

The number of deaths in New York city is 10,200 in 2 years; the whole population, 200 thousand, will die in how many years?

A human body, if baked until all moisture is evaporated, is reduced in weight as 1 to 10; a body that weighs 100 pounds living, will weigh how much when dry?

A boy works every day; how many are there left?

OF FAST OR LOOSE

Now I'll tell you how
To knit a tight knot
In a bit of cloth
And then undo it
With a word or two.

You need to know how
To cinch it just so
With a touch of stealth
To keep the sweet spot
As free as it's taut.

You ought to show how
It's just what it's not
At a certain length
Until you start to
Utter your whatnot.

You must know by now
A dark art is but
A piece of the truth
You hide in plain sight
To do what you do

With a bit of show
And an oath or two
As if it were caught
As you let it out
With your bated breath.

TRICKERATION

Cab Calloway, Cotton Club (1931)

Rhythm, look what you went and done.
Rhythm, you are the guilty one.
The sneaky one, the snaky one,
The breakneck one, the hell-bent one.
Rhythm, you are the guilty one.

Rhythm, you are a loaded gun.
Rhythm, you've left me all undone.
Rhythm, you are the slinky one,
The funky one, the freaky one,
The harum one, the scarum one.

Rhythm, I took you one-on-one.
Now look at what you've gone and done.
Rhythm, you are the righteous one,
The badass one, the brass-balls one.
Rhythm, you are the one who's won.

Rhythm, I am the broken one,
The token done-in chosen one.
Rhythm, you are the golden one
To everyone, the only one
Who showed me how it should be done.

Rhythm, you call us and we run
To something new under the sun.
Rhythm, you are the dodgy one,
The deadly one, the guilty one.
Rhythm, look what you've gone and done.

ERRAND

Consider it done: a left-handed rake
And a broom to match, a sky hook,
A neck tourniquet, a can of striped paint
And the keys to the oarlocks,
A pail of steam, a bucket of smoke.

And for good measure, a pipe-stretcher,
A brick-bender, a hole-remover,
A ball of tartan yarn, a boiled icicle,
A Cyrillic pencil, a glass hammer,
And an extra bubble for the spirit-level.

And while I'm at it, a long weight
(I'll cool my heels while they look
Out back), a little rainbow oil,
And what the heck, maybe another
Box of sparks for the shape-shifter.

And no, I won't forget to wind up
The compass and unring the bell
(I'm a nonesuch at this sort of stuff),
Just as soon as I scare up a brass magnet,
Some elbow grease, and a fist pump.

Look here, I'm ticking it all off
On foolscap: hens' teeth, a mare's nest,
A basket case, a left-handed spanner,
A brace of snipe, a barrel of folderol,
And nobody need be the wiser.

THE MAGIC MOVING PICTURE BOOK

London: Bliss, Sands & Co. (1898)

Wheels turn! Fish swim! Fire burns! Water flows!

In an inner pocket will be found a Transparency; all that need be done is to
follow the instructions printed beneath each scene.

Push up and down up and down slow as you can to create motion.

Magic Circles. Magic Squares. The Serpentine Dancer. The Snow Storm.

Now vastly improved—simplicity itself, but a novelty the inventor has worked
on like a Trojan in pursuit of perfection.

See that the ring finger works like a pivot; note the many changes of pattern on
The Changeable Tint that can be seen.

The Water Mill. The Mortar Mill. The Traction Engine. The Aquarium.

Place the star on the Transparency over the star above the picture—the smoke
will pour out of the funnel and the wheels revolve.

Observe the movement in the fishes' fins as the water ripples over them.

The Volcano. The House on Fire. The Steamboat. The Three Fountains.

You will notice the smoke and flames shoot upwards as the lava streams down
the mountain and the eruption is reflected in the ocean.

Observe the dancing waves and the spinning balls, the windblown snow, the
rooms ablaze, the showgirl coiling, the pluming steam.

See that the Transparency lies flat against the paper: star on star, the pattern stirring into being, the fine lines milling, whirling, flaring, churning.

Slow as you can up and down up and down: magic, motion, combustion, illusion, wheels swimming, water burning, fire flowing, pages turning.

THE STUDY OF BUTTERFLIES

Henry Walter Bates, *The Naturalist on the River Amazons* (1863)

At Ega, on the Upper Amazons, over 500 new species by his count.

Within 10 minutes' tramp of his cabin, 18 types of true swallowtail alone.

No fact could speak so plainly for the surpassing abundance and vitality
   of the place,

Though no brute tally can convey an adequate notion of the beauty and variety

In form and color an intrepid collector encounters in these parts.

To them then he devotes special care and attention, certain there is none better

For making clear the constant changes all creatures must undergo to go on.

Here is where the real allure lies. See how he can array an entire tribe

Side by side under glass to show how every inkling of variation
   and succession

From generation to generation, each tint and crimp and dappled scallop,

Each fiery streak, each mock eyespot, must be in keeping with
   what's fitting.

Let us say then that on these luminous membranes are written, as surely and
   distinctly as on

Any leaves of law or revelation, the unfolding story our newfound field of
   study is only

Now uncovering wing by wing: the secret history of every living thing.

ON A SHAKER ADMONITION

All should be so trustworthy, that locks and keys shall be needless.

Needless, useless, pointless, moot: stripped of every honest purpose,
　　nothing so haplessly worthless now, so meaningless.

Needless, needless: the deadbolt, the strongbox, the padlock
　　lolling from the tall spiked gate, the little metal teeth
all jingle-jangling mindlessly on their rusting ring, the all too obtuse
　　fitfulness of pin and tumbler, every chain known to man.

All melted down for scrap: the whole clanking, tinkling, delirious mess
　　spaded into the pitiless furnace for our trusty smiths
to put to good use, all that glorious blazing gloop walloped anew into
　　buckles, skillets, wind chimes, windup toys, more spades.

Needless, worthless, baseless, daft: the locket, the lockbox, the lockers
　　slam-banging in the winless locker room, the secret
hasp in the desk or the case to trip for the stash, the fireproof safe,
　　the bulletproof vest, the chastity belt, the countless
stacks of patents for atomic bombproof vaults kept under lock and key,
　　all gone the way of relics, ruins, fossils, flesh.

Useless, useless as useless gets: the dupe under the doormat, the blanks
　　on their hooks, the plink of trinkets (church key, poker chip,
bronzed trilobite) from this or that set, the cutting kit's merciless shriek
　　in the back of the shop, the brassy tang on the tongue
when wrangling hands free in a breathless rush to slip in or out, the endless
　　cat and mouse of masters and skeletons laid to rest at last.

The heartless turnkey, the nerveless safecracker, the latchkey kid
　　scared shitless, the relentlessly dauntless escape artist
trussed in shackles and manacles in shot after shot: who among us
　　could even make up stuff so specious, so spurious?

No cutpurse to fleece us, no jackboot to roust us, no half-assed excuse
        to detain us, remand us, debase us, reform us,
no iron fist or invisible hand to quash or unleash us, no righteous
        crusade to destroy us to save us: just us, just us.

All of us no longer shiftless, feckless, careless, faithless: no losses to cut,
        no charges to press, nothing to witness, nothing to confess,
no one to cast into the wilderness, no caste to dispossess, no shamefulness,
        no shamelessness, no cease and desist, no underhandedness
under duress, nothing to peer into or peep at with a flickering eyelash,
        each cloudless passing hour lusting after less and less.

Should be, so be it: so trustworthy, so noteworthy, so rock-steady,
        so truth-hungry, so war-weary, so far from foolhardy,
so otherworldly already, no guest or ghost would guess that any of us
        were ever less than blameless, faultless, spotless, blessed.

Needless, useless, pointless, crap: the polygraph, the wiretap, the clink of cuffs,
        the accordion gate, the ankle bracelet, the honeycombed spy cams,
the blueprints for the deluxe panopticon, all that superfluous refuse shipped off
        to the pawn shop, the swap meet, the flea mart, the boundless
county dump, the bottomless dustbin of clueless things past, all dead as
        the doornail that held fast against the hopeless crush of us.

No senseless wishfulness, no useless ruthlessness, no goods to get on us
        to bust or traduce us, no clauses to bind us, no cause
for redress, no one on the loose, on the make, on the case, nothing for us
        to jimmy or pick, nothing gone missing, not a thing amiss,
no No Tell Motel, no Big House, no Pale beyond us, no tragic chorus in a rumpus
        over the worst in us getting the best of us in spite of us,

just all of us lapsing less and less regardless how rootless, witless, gutless, pissed,
        all that thankless cussed nonsense now behind us: just us, just us.

SHERPA SONG

Your rope, my rope. My tracks,
Your steps. Beneath my feet,
The drop. Around my waist,
Your weight. On my back,
Your stuff, my yoke, the works.

Your pace, my pace. My task,
Your quest. Underfoot, crack
After crack, the ice, the ice.
Above and beyond, our route,
The world's roof, a roost of mist.

Over one shoulder, a yelp
Downslope, a whoop back up:
My jabber, your babble, our heart-
To-heart in the heat of our assault
On the last face, pitch by pitch.

Up top, tapped out: your breath,
My breath, gasp for gasp, our
Dragon clouds. Out there, nowhere
But here, where air comes dear:
No far, no near, the end of all roads.

Your neck, my neck. Your cross,
My wind horse. Your mule,
My ass: try soulmate, your muse,
My own man. Under my mask,
My real mask, your open book.

YOGI GLOSA

I never said most of the things I said.
Half the things I said, I never said them.
I didn't really say everything I said,
But you say I said them so I said them.

I never said half the things you say I said
Unless I said them because you read them.
It's almost as if no one heard me say
If you can't imitate him, don't copy him.

I never said most of the things I said,
But never say never is what I say.
When you come to a fork in the road,
Take it. The future ain't what it used to be.

I've said it plain, and I'll say it again:
I never said most of the things I said.
As I've always said, it's catch as catch can
If you say stuff with my voice in your head.

Who says a man is as good as his word?
Half the lies they tell about me aren't true.
I couldn't have said all those things I said,
But sometimes I say I did anyway.

Maybe I said what you say I said on cue,
Or maybe you just read my mind instead.
It gets late early out here, it's déjà vu
All over again. Was it something I said?

It ain't over till it's over. So said
Some soothsayer, so let's say I'm him.
I never said most of the things I said,
But if I didn't say them, who said them?

Ninety percent of the game is half mental.
You can observe a lot by watching. See?
Say what you will, but I say we say uncle.
If the world were perfect, it wouldn't be.

SAND MAN

Sand and nothing but sand, rainbow sand
found only at a certain river-bend in sand-
stone stained by iron, the finest sand
around if what you have in mind is a sand-
bottle keepsake, a design or scene in sand.

Sand sifted grain by grain: red sand,
blue sand, green sand, mounds of sand
you can blend into saffron and golden sand
if you were deaf and dumb and saw in sand
what never before has been seen in sand.

Sand in a winding crimson band, sand
in an answering ebony strand, sand
in serpentine diamonds and vanes: sand
and nothing but sand on sand, as if sand
could have been ink and silk, not sand.

Sand by the quarter-teaspoon, flaxen sand
on ashen sand, ginger sand then raven sand
tamped firm and plumb, poring over the sand
for a thousand hours or more so the sand
stands for all a man can find sound in sand.

Sand on sand, sandwiched in sand:
no handy glue or paste to bind the sand,
no dye of any kind to gild the sand,
nothing but the true sheen of the sand
to lend pleasing dimension to the sand.

And nothing in the stoppered jar but sand
bound fast by sand, fine bands of sand
unfurling into streaming banners of sand
bordered by braided chevrons of sand
blooming into spangled bouquets of sand.

And when you've learned to inscribe the sand
in a flowing hand, signing a name in sand
that flickers like flame when the vial of sand
turns round and round, it can be *Mary's* sand
and *Henry's* sand, a fond token of sand,

and when you've learned to render sand
into snakeskin and tartan a pinch of sand
at a time, the pattern in the sand
withstanding the pressure of the sand,
then anything you can imagine in sand,

sand can become: a verdant garland of sand
wound round an urn, an amber wave of sand
at harvest time, sand moon and stars, sand
stars and stripes, azure sand and silver sand
fanned into a wingspan on a shield of sand

and sand alone, an American eagle in sand
brandishing a pearl-handled staff in stern sand
talons to unwind a sandy Old Glory, the sand
in its fiery eye such a pinpoint glint of sand
some even see a mirroring gleam in the sand.

And then a line in the sand, a sand
horizon without end, and where sand
meets skyline in the heartland of sand,
a house, a horse, an iron horse of sand
trailing a commanding plume of smoky sand,

and where sand makes waves as plains of sand
give way to unscrolling lowlands of sand,
a steamboat plying a wending river of sand
under grandstanding thunderheads of sand
to round out the sepia wonderland of sand.

And when one was done, you ran sand
from hand to hand until soon the sand
called a newfound creation to mind: sand
steeples and teepees in one surround, sand
farmlands and happy hunting grounds, sand

and nothing but sand for light and shade, sand
sifted grain by grain for near and far, sand
sown upside down with a homemade wand, sand
taking the measure of all things as only sand
can when you see the world in a handful of sand.

And to answer the slander that your works in sand
had to be some sleight of hand, a dram of sand
might be smashed on demand—a burst of sand, sand
schooners and rosebuds blown to oblivion, sand
and blinding sand alone, sand and nothing but sand.

THE RUBAIYAT OF OMAR AQTA

Two tasks, O master court calligrapher,
Two tasks at the far ends of your tether.
Bring two Qurans to the Great Tamerlane:
The smallest on earth, the biggest ever.

First every word the prophet handed down
In script so deft, so miniscule, so fine,
All the teachings fit on a signet ring
To slip on the finger of your grand khan.

And now every verse from the angel's tongue
On pages as vast as cranes on the wing,
A volume so mighty, breaking so much ground,
You'll need an oxcart to trundle it along.

One's ringing lines smaller than grains of sand;
One's lavish brushstrokes the largest ever found:
Two matchless versions faithfully set down
In one inspired scribe's surpassing hand.

O Omar, you are more than your iron sovereign
Could bargain for in a driven minion.
If you fail to please him with your small wonder,
Let's have a revision one can scan from heaven.

PAINTER'S WIFE'S ISLAND

Sir Walter Raleigh, *The History of the World*

No woman's an island,
But this one's hers and hers alone:
A speck in the straits way off
To itself, a mote on the map
For her to call her own.

"A pretty jest," the poet locked up
In the Tower lets it be known,
A beaut he fell hard for himself
On one long return trip round
The Horn, combing the horizon.

All for her, her promised land
That won't be found, one fond one
For the trouble and strife,
One deft flick of a brush-tip
To mark the spot she has in mind.

Here's her back of beyond, her own
Haunt on the chart, here in the gap
Between hearsay and herself,
A one-of-a-kind no-man's-land
For her alone to maroon on.

To each her own, but this one
Beats all: her story history, the map
Long gone, the lay of her land
A nowhere where her secret life
Lives on, hers and hers alone.

MAMIHLAPINATAPAI

Meaning, in Yaghan, the wordless yet meaningful look between two people
    who want to begin something but are both reluctant to start.

Meaning, in other words, that moment of silence that says so much more about why
    we're speechless than all that would be lost in translation.

Meaning, you've said a mouthful, stranger, maybe we should get to know each other better.

Meaning, next time you're down in Tierra del Fuego, let's say we take a meeting,
    if you know what I mean.

Meaning, maybe we could make beautiful music together by saying nothing,
    if only you, not me, would get things going.

Meaning, easy for you to say, word maven, so why oh why don't you make the first move.

Meaning, what in the world are we doing, doing nothing when we could be
    speaking in tongues in the land of fire?

Which doesn't mean that any of this has to make sense, no matter how momentous
    it may sound, no matter how much

It may have meant when our eyes met, no matter how much more it would mean
    if I were to give you my word

In my meandering way that one day we'll be finishing each other's sentences.

Which might then mean that you and me weren't meant to be, unless in the meantime
    word gets around, all the way back around Cape Horn,

Where it's said there's now only one surviving native speaker left to tell us
    why we're hanging fire.

Meaning, if you will, the world is full of words that are meaningless unless they say something unmistakable about us.

Meaning, more or less, you can go to the ends of the earth and still be at a loss over what to say about what just passed between us.

KAMA SUTRA ERRATA

For *Crouching Tiger* read *Curling Angel.*

For *blow of a boar* read *blow of a bull.*

For *hard* read *harder,* for *fast* read *faster*

Harder faster harder harder faster.

In "Of Love Marks," it should be the Broken Cloud,

Not the Coral and Jewels, impressed on the breast.

In the Index of Embraces, the list should include

The Top, the Tongs, the Swing, the Treasure Chest.

Retraction: dipping the tip in goat's milk won't work.

Correction: the Mare's Trick is the master stroke.

In "On Sirens," consult the Congress of Crows

Before attempting the Sporting of Swallows.

For *moon* read *moan,* for *possession, abandon.*

All other errors are yours and yours alone.

SONG OF NOTHING

Guilhem IX (ca. 1070–1127), *Farai un vers de dreit rein*

I'll make a song out of nothing at all.
It's not about me or any living soul,
Nothing to do with lost youth or some doll
Or anything under the sun.
I dreamt it up last night behind the wheel
Waiting for the light to turn.

I have no clue how I came to be born.
I take no pleasure and I feel no pain.
I'm not a stranger and I'm not your friend.
What makes me tick is not my call—
Go ask the shadow that slipped on my skin
Out there beyond the pale.

I can't be certain if I'm asleep or awake.
Somebody tell me and make it quick.
Sometimes it's like my heart's about to crack
From a wound with no name,
But you won't hear a gripe out of this sad sack,
So help me Doubting Tom!

I'm sick to death and my nerves are shot,
But all I know is what I hear on the street.
I'm looking for a shrink who'll set me straight,
But where to start?
If there's a cure for what ails me—sweet.
If not, no sweat.

I have a lover, but I don't know her.
We've never even met. Why bother?
She's done me no good, but no harm either
So far as I can tell—
She's not a housewife or a home-wrecker,
Call her what you will.

We've never hooked up, but I swear she's the one.
I don't get my hopes up, so she never lets me down.
When we're not an item I get by just fine,
Don't lose any sleep.
I've got another flame with charm to burn
And she's just my type.

That's my ditty—sweet nothings for no one.
I'll inscribe it to a certain someone
Who'll croon it to my silver-tongued twin
On the red-eye to Lotusland
And back will come the key to my fortune
In an unknown hand.

HANETSUKI

Badminton at first blush, but wait—no net.
To hone your timing you had to team up:
Tapping the shuttlecock back and forth without
Letting it drop, *tick-tock, bip-bap.*

You were a girl at court. You grew adept.
The feathered soapberry you'd deftly flick
With your little painted battledore darted like
A dragonfly, a charm against mosquito bites.

Was it bad form then to want to do best?
The one who let the winged seed bite the dust
Had to wear a black daub of ink on her cheek.

So turn the other one. When I click the link
On the floating world of your woodblock print,
You've still got the knack, and no one has lost.

KABOCHA-TOLI

Ball's up—a streaming plain of naked men
Going at it like there's no tomorrow,
Scrum after broiling scrum, clan against clan
Several hundred strong, the blow-by-blow
So smashmouth you can hear the crack of shin
On shin, hipbone smacking off hipbone—
And somewhere on the sidelines a white man
Scratching notes and sketches, taking it all down.

Who won? Who knows. But here's Tullock-chish-ko
Striking a pose, He Who Drinks the Juice of the Stone—
None better in his nation, a born superstar, chin
In the air and torso thrown back so Catlin can show
How to wield your ball-sticks webbed with deerskin
As a plume of horsehair fountains from your tailbone.

SLOW BURN

The dopey one's gone and done it again
And here's another nice mess you're in—
All widdershins among the smithereens
And sodden with something's oozing remains,
Your britches in ruins, your bowler stove in,
Your collar waggling like a broken wing—
But you've always known, you've always known
The world does nothing but do you wrong,
So what can a silent clown do now but turn
A moonface to us on the far side of the lens
As the noodling organ keeps rubbing it in,
Since when can any meltdown or mad scene
Hold a candle to a mug that's a study in
Every smoldering pang that goes unspoken?

FOLEY ROOM

Pinches of sea salt kneaded between gloved fingers
Plucky orphan stealing away over new-fallen snow

Snap open an umbrella, worry a ball of cellophane, repeat
One by one burning all the secret letters up

Sand or sawdust in a gunnysack, *smack* across a cinder block
Was he pushed or did he fall?

Damp palms rubbing a rubber balloon right into the mic
Pleasure craft or ghost ship scraping the dock in the dark

Cornflakes in a shoebox, first one fist then another
Her late ex-lover tromping off over the boneyard's dead leaves

Clop-clop of hollow coconuts, *clip-clock* of plumber's friends
Horses, more horses, the posse making tracks

Stacked metro phonebooks *whump whump* off a tabletop
Right cross, uppercut, haymaker, down goes the champ

Tap sticks tap sticks, thunk blocks thunk blocks
Down the steps, out the back, his old man in pursuit

Listen, it's an art: getting everything in sync
making it so all the goings-on go on on cue

Gravel pit, grass pit, marble slab, bin of planks
Slog, trudge, skulk, bolt, swan about, hop to it, get lost

Wrenches, hinges, matches, hubcaps, bedsheets, spoons
Creaks, rustles, clanks, sparks, things going smash

Slapslapslap go the garden gloves *Slapslap*
> *In and out flits the bat, the bat, the bat that might not even be a bat*

Unscrewing slowly over the john the jumbo mason jar
> *The hatch of the mother ship opening opening inch by inch*

Kissing and kissing the back of your own hand
> *Kissing and kissing the one the only one yes yes at last in the end*

TABLE

J. Prevost, *Clever & Pleasant Inventions, Part One* (1584)

To Start a Motion That Shall Last a Very Long Time

To Cut a String, Which Shall Later Be Found to Be Quite Whole

To Make a Knife Jump Out of a Pot without Touching It

To Make Forms Such as Cities, Mountains, and Other Things Appear in a Vial Full of Water

To Discover in a Pleasant Manner Who Is the Greatest Man of All the Company

To Be Able to Guess Three Objects Which Three People Have Taken and Hidden

To Make a Light Be Seen Moving through the Room at Night, Not without Causing Some Alarm

To Make Some Little Grotesque Figures Dance Prettily on the Surface of a Sieve to the Sound of Bells

How You May Know the Number That Someone Has Thought Of

How You May Break a Stone with a Blow of Your Fist

How It May Be Made to Seem That You Have Your Tongue Pierced Through with an Awl

Another Method of Restraining Someone, This Time with a Ring or Brass Loop

Another Easier and Shorter Method to Discover a Number Someone Has Thought Of

To Write When Necessary on Glass, without a Diamond

CARTON FANTASTIQUE

Jean-Eugène Robert-Houdin, *Confidences d'un prestidigitateur* (1858)

The secret is to love your own illusion.
The trick is to live in your imagination.

My aim was to save the best for last.
My plan was to give away nothing at first.

My life was an open secret up to then.
My first love was secondhand legerdemain.

The task was to see if I passed my own test.
The first step was to obscure my dark past.

The first thing you'd see was a man about town
Flourishing a trim portfolio of finest calfskin.

The trick is make an illusion last.
The secret is to leave an impression first.

The last thing such a thing could contain
Was a cage of doves and a smoking pan,

But those first neat tricks could only mean
My labors of love were far from done.

The test is to see if you can trust the rest.
Let me root around even deeper first.

The trick is never to call your attention
To the secret passion behind the pattern.

My case must conceal a short list at the most.
The thing looks like it's been collecting dust.

The trick is to look as stunned as anyone.
The secret is making your own head spin.

Just when it's certain that all must be lost,
Look what I'll fish from my sheaf at long last.

My act is complete. Bring the curtain down on
My greatest sensation, my very own son.

INDIAN ROPE TRICK

A rope rises up into the air.
A boy climbs up the rope.
Up at the top, he disappears.
The rope stays put. The boy's not there.
A clap of the hands. The rope
Drops in a heap. The boy's nowhere.

The man wears a turban and a beard.
The boy's a street arab, all in rags.
There they are, in the public square.
Up goes the rope. The man gives the word.
Up goes the boy, shaking a leg.
The rope goes limp. The boy's not there.

They say sometimes he reappears.
The bearded one goes up the rope
In hot pursuit, knife in his teeth.
Body parts drop with a pulpy thump
Out of the mist, but the boy cheats death.
Up he pops, no worse for wear.

Read all about it. Here's the scoop.
They say the rope must be a prop.
Some report a puff of smoke.
Some say it must be staged at dusk.
One sahib remembers feeling queer
From something pungent in the air.

A broth of a boy, barefoot and shorn.
A man with a brow like polished wood.
There they were, in the great bazaar.
The rope was a snake. It hung in the air
Above the throng. At his master's word
The boy groped up and then he was gone.

You whip your rope with dapper flair.
You let it go and it floats like a charm.
You bark at your boy in an ancient tongue.
You show the rabble how it's done.
You clench your shiv and go after him,
Flouting the laws that all hold dear.

The rope must have a mind of its own.
The boy has got to fly the coop.
Maroon him midway to the moon
Beyond the dark side of a doubt.
Abracadabra—I make as I speak.
Walk the talk or the trick won't work.

Send me up your spellbound rope.
Wipe me off the face of the earth.
Make it look like there's no hope
Before you bring me back to life.
I fall to pieces. I have no prayer.
My fate is neither here nor there.

Dupe us, shaman. Rope us in.
Boy, go missing. Make us gape.
Here we are, creating a stir.
It's up to us to talk you up,
Suspending disbelief again.
The truth is hanging by a hair.

The rope climbs halfway to the stars.
Up at the top, the boy disappears.
The traveler's tale grows like a vine.
See if you can top this one:
The rope's coiled up, the boy's not there.
Rub your eyes: that's him right here.

THE LION'S BRIDE

Now the man-killer roars on cue.
Now the brass band begins to wheeze.
Then the fire-eaters clear their throats,
And then the gaslights sputter out.
And now the great beast paces and fumes,
Switching his tail now and then.

Now the damsel ripples the wings.
Then the spot bathes her up and down.
And now there's a whiff of holy smoke,
And now the swell of an opera march.
Then you can taste the heat in the tent.
Now the sacred rite can commence.

And now behind that frothing veil
The fair lass must be swallowing hard—
For now she's taking her own sweet time
Wafting past the crush like a swan,
Leaving a snail-track as her train
Glisters along in the ogling beam.

And now we ask the faint of heart
To hold on to your smelling salts.
You've seen the banns all over town
And now you'll witness the solemn vows.
Don't look now, but there's no escape:
The cage yaws open, then in she slips

As if she were a roosting dove.
And now they're going to tie the knot,
And then till death shall do them part
They'll swear to be true through thick and thin.
And then you'll know where you were when
The law of the jungle took a honeymoon.

And now the bridegroom bellows again,
And now he's rampant, and then a scream
Rattles the china for leagues around.
O little lamb, you're a goner now—
But no, he's tearing off his skin
And lo and behold, now he's a man

In velveteen tails, bowing low.
And now if I told you exactly how
The jaw-dropping thing was done, what then?
That was then and this is now.
The switch was over before it began.
Love conquers all, all over again.

ILLUSION

Unless we plant our faith in things unseen,
Everything will be exactly what it seems.

I have here a seed, an ordinary seed
In every way, as you can plainly see.

See how I simply give it a good squeeze.
You can see I have nothing up my sleeve.

If my lips were sealed, my pip would sleep
Until the seas dry up, sleek in its sheath,

Seeking out nothing, but as soon as I speak
My secret stave, see how it begins to seethe.

See what I mean? My unsung little seed's
A seedling now, springing a sidelong seam.

You can see how smartly it gets up to speed—
A sweep of my kerchief, and it's on a spree.

Now watch as I slip my sweet under a sheet
In a teacup of reeking sod so it can steep

By degrees until a shearing strain can be seen
In keeping with the creed that says a seed

Has to be a steely creeping thing to spread
The word that shade begins in spears of sheen.

Now I'll strip off the scrim so you can see
Why I never plead or wheedle with my seed.

See how it's shooting up in one strapping skein
As serene as you please under its own steam.

Another word in code, another shake of the sheet—
Behold all the buds and now leaves by the sheaf.

It's that kind of breed: not one to be swayed
By a bleeding heart or a reaper seeing red,

No thin reed ripped from the forcing shed
Or some sheepish weed by the old mill stream.

There now, you see? All your seed needs to seize
The day is your deepest esteem, sight unseen.

One sure thing leads to another when you see
What a seed can be if you believe in a seed.

Yes indeed, those are sun-ripe orbs you see,
Out of season but still the bee's knees, no sweat.

If you saw this feat up on the silver screen
You'd say you spied some shady plot or scheme,

But here you've got yourself a ringside seat
To guarantee you've seen just what you've seen.

What do you see when you see a seed? I see
A streak of green need, a great leap under siege,

A new field decreed, a spade stood in good stead,
Weeping tree rings to read, fair seedtime redeemed

By the sea change of a seed, the striptease of a seed,
The stagecraft, the street cred, the prestige of a seed,

The all-seeing stem-winding scene-stealing stampede
Over common ground when seed meets winged seed

Until it seems all the world's a teeming seedbed.
I see the forest, I see the trees, I see a cloud-seeder

Drawing a bead. I see the herb-yielding seed,
The fruit whose seed is in itself, the date stone freed

To sow its own kind again in the sands. I see seeds
Split and sprout where sibyls fear to tread, I see

Wild oats in cahoots with the salt of the earth, I see
The tools and tricks of the trade side by side

When I see a seed slip through the needle's eye.
I see what a seer sees when she sees the shroud

Stripped away between things seen and unseen.
I see stardust and moonshine when I see a seed

Doing whatever it takes for a seed to succeed.
I see a sedulous spirit to conjure by, the shrewd

Stuff of sheer feel no sorcery can supersede,
A deed yet to be done, something still to be said.

TUMBLER

Handspring handspring handspring handspring
Backflip backflip backflip stick

Handspring handspring handspring roundoff
Running start layout whipsnap double back

Here you are there you go getting loose warming up
For the pharaoh the emperor the games the big meet

You sprint and plant you hit your spot you flip you flop
You pick yourself up you dust yourself off

In your prime nothing on buck naked or just about
Tank top short shorts bright crest a velvet stripe

Handspring handspring handspring full tilt breakneck
Hotshot buzz cut bopahunk bust a gut holy crap

You leap you bound you get good air you go all out
You rock you roll no flies on you no moss no rust

Showmen stuntmen lettermen he-men acrobats jocks
Six-pack abs thunder-thighs hardbody ripped

Your turn now champ one long line going all the way back
Hieroglyph amphora agate type Kodachrome YouTube clip

In a troupe on a team for bread fame love sport
Go for it gym rat keep it up keep it up

Pecs delts traps quads wasp waist barrel chest
Backflip backflip arse over ears reverse double tuck

Knossos Memphis Shandong Circus Maximus Muscle Beach
Trojans Spartans Turners Saltimbanques All City All State

You twist you turn you spin you land one thump
In the square on the strand over spotlit scarlet mats

Back in training rounding into form Elysium at last
Phenom young turk jumping jack no slips no breaks

All a blur who's who how to zoom in how to pick you out
Back in the day long before the fact nobody's dad yet

The body a coil a lever a mainspring a flying machine
A breaking wave a streaking flaring wheeling thing

There you are here you go on your toes blasting off
In an arena named for a war hero a chieftain a saint

How to vault a bull wow the crowd top the field no sweat
You know the ancient wisecrack practice practice practice

And now let's see you do it on the long horse
Bull rush cat spring wingfoot snakehips lionheart

Old school breathe deep make it look like a walk
In the park a piece of cake arms in a V upthrust

Brushstrokes keepsakes snapshots ghost by ghost
How can the son lay the old man to rest

Handspring handspring handspring tuck pike stick
Over and over O throwback blur don't stop don't stop

ON THE SPECTACLES

Martial, *Liber Spectaculorum*

Now see for yourself
How the myth comes to life:
The king's wife who balled a bull
Here in your arena for real.
You better believe it, Chief.

***

Humble as you please,
The tusker that broke the ox's back
Shambles to your box, goes
Down on his knees. It's no act,
Boss, he too knows who's who.

***

Don't look now, but here come
The informers, the tellers of lies
On parade, and our stadium
Can't hold them all. Beat it, stoolies:
The bitter end is yours this time.

***

A hotshot troupe of sea nymphs
Sporting in naked formation: look,
A trident, an anchor, a ship, the star
Seamen delight in. Who dreamed up
Such tricks? A goddess, some bright girl.

***

To see the big old bull
Swooped up on the spot,
Swept away aloft, goes to show
How to slay your full house:
Not by art but faithful brute force.

BALLYHOO

Zat Zam can sling a knife like no one can.
Zat Zam can zing a handful at a time.
They say you can hear the steel sing
When Zat Zam is hurling in sterling form.

Zat Zam can trepan the queen of diamonds
At twenty paces with a blindfold on.
Zat Zam can silhouette a sweet young thing
With shivs that quiver as they hit home.

Zat Zam cannot turn water into wine
But he can make a knife take wing.
While you're catching Z's, Zat Zam is working
On striking you dumb for his star turn.

Zat Zam can zero in like no man can.
Zat Zam can find his range in any ring.
The line forms here for his right-hand maiden
All but impaled all up and down.

They say his name is like the sound
His knives make when they do their thing.
Zat-zam! Zat-zam! Zat-zam! Zat-zam!
His hand is quicker than your tongue.

Zat Zam is a showman's showman's showman.
Zat Zam once performed before the King.
Zat Zam knocked 'em dead with the Ringling brethren.
Zat Zam has never not been in his prime.

Zat Zam could have been an Aztec chieftain
If he had been born in another time.
Zat Zam is a full-blooded Indian
And one hundred percent American.

Zat Zam and Zat Zam's little woman
Barnstorm as the dazzling duo the Zat Zams.
She's the one who leaves behind her form
In spread-eagled daggers when the deed is done.

Zat Zam does not go in for humdrum flimflam.
Next to Zat Zam, Zorro is all thumbs.
They say you haven't seen anything
Until you drop everything for Zat Zam.

No pinup siren ever bought the farm
By cutting a fine figure for Zat Zam.
Zat Zam can count on his golden arm
To draw the line between life and limb.

Zat Zam throws every atom of his being
Into showing you how it's done—*Shazam!*
You'll swear you've just seen a djinn in buckskin.
You can hear the whizbang right there in his name.

ZAT ZAM should be emblazoned on a zeppelin
As he's zooming to the zenith of his fame.
Zat-zam! Zat-zam! Zat-zam! Zat-zam!
He aims to amaze or his name's not Zat Zam.

BLUE MAN SONG

Diagnosis: Argyria
Cause of Death: Pneumonia
Bellevue Hospital 1923

All I can tell you is what I told you before.
It's getting to where I can barely get air.
My heart keeps pounding like I'm a locked door.
I don't know how much more I can bear.
But whatever I've got, it's got nothing to do
With the shade of my hide. I was born this blue.

Call me a freak, but I know what I know.
It must be something else that's laid me low.
I've always been tall, I've always been thin,
I've always been the bluest of men.
Blue tongue, blue lips, toes and fingers all blue,
And the whites of my eyes—see, they're blue too.

Didn't you know the circus was in town?
Haven't you heard about Barnum's Blue Man?
Now that you've got me stretched out and stripped down,
Can't you see that I'm blue to the bone?
You must not know who you're talking to
If you're saying I'm dying to be blue.

All my pals told me, up there in Bellevue
They'll know what to do, or nobody will.
But I'm starting to think you don't have a clue
How to heal a fellow who feels like hell.
Whatever I've caught, it's got nothing to do
With my ballyhooed hue. I've always been blue.

Go ahead, take it all down one more time.
No, I've never set foot in an old silver mine.
No, I'm not some kind of a darkroom bum.
No, I've never gulped down one bullet or coin.
No, no, no, it's just like I've been telling you:
When my maker made me, he made me true blue.

I don't have a thing to get off my chest.
I was a blue babe at my mother's breast.
I grew up blue, and until I drop dead
Being blue is how I'll make my bread.
They say even my shadow throws a blue glow,
Somewhere between azure and indigo.

Since when is being so blue such a sin?
Out on the Midway, I've blended right in.
There's Rubber Man and there's the Wild Man,
And me in between, serene in my skin.
It must be the pox or some foul ague
That's got me in knots right out of the blue.

I must have heard every sick joke in the book
About blue ruin, blue moons, and blue balls.
I've been called an ape-man, a spade, a spook,
And told to bunk down in stables and stalls.
But it's a new one on me to be told to rue
The dark day I knew I had to be blue.

I've crisscrossed the country from sea to sea,
Staking my claim on this peerless blue sheen.
Way out West, I make the bluebirds turn green.
In Texas bluebonnets look daggers at me.
In Dixie the bluesmen give me my due
By riffing on how I got so black-and-blue.

If you say this is it, if the end is near,
I'll sign whatever you want me to sign.
You can crack me open and lay me bare,
You can pickle my parts to see if they shine.
Do with me whatever you want to do
So long as you don't rule I was too blue.

I'm fading fast now, but you've got to see—
If I wasn't blue, I wouldn't be me.
I've always been long, I've always been lean,
When I dream I dream in aquamarine.
Believe me, I'm one of the happy few
Who don't need a strange brew to be blue.

I don't know what to say to docs like you
Who see red when they see a man who's blue.
I know how it looks, but I tell you it's true:
There was never a day I wasn't blue.
Before my last gasp, look and see how blue
A man gets to be when he's got to be blue.

ZOO HAS A PYGMY TOO MANY
Does Anybody Want This Orphan Boarder? He Does Not
Bite, He Does Not Vote, His Manners, Though Various, Are Mild

BUSHMAN SHARES A CAGE WITH BRONX PARK APES
Some Laugh Over His Antics, but Many Are Not Pleased

A PYGMY AMONG PRIMATES
One of the "Bantams" of the African Race in the Zoological Park

LIVELY ROW OVER PYGMY
Colored Ministers to Act; The Pygmy Has an Orang-outang as a
Companion Now & Their Pranks Delight the Bronx Crowds

TOPICS OF THE TIMES
Send Him Back to the Woods

TOPICS OF THE TIMES
The Pigmy Is Not the Point

THE MAYOR WON'T HELP TO FREE CAGED PYGMY
Refers Negro Clergy Offended by Man and Monkey Show
to the Zoological Society; Crowd Annoys the Dwarf

BUSHMAN SAYS CIVILIZATION IS ALL WITCHCRAFT
On Exhibition in the Bronx, He Rules Monkey House by
Jungle Dread; Wants to Go Home to Buy Him a Wife

BENGA TRIES TO KILL
Pygmy Slashes at Keeper Who Objected to His Garb

COLORED ORPHAN HOME GETS THE PYGMY
He Has a Room to Himself & May Smoke If He Likes

HOPE FOR OTA BENGA

If Little, He's No Fool; Won't Be an Entrée Here, but His Chief
in the Congo May Die Soon & the Custom Is a Cannibal Feast

BENGA AT HIPPODROME

Pygmy Meets His Old Friend, the Baby Elephant, Giving Out Programmes

OTA BENGA NOW A REAL COLORED GENTLEMAN

Little African Pygmy Being Taught Ways of the Civilized World
at Long Island Colored Orphan Asylum

A WORD FOR BENGA

Prof. Verner, African Traveler & American Sponsor,
Asks New York Not to Spoil His Friend, the Bushman

September–October 1906

SOLO

He pointed to a picture of a coffin and told me, "Play that."
—YUSEF LATEEF

So there you were, all ready to blow—
But where were the bars, the keys,
The staves, the bare bones of the tune?
And what's with this black box
Where your changes should go?

So much for last night's slow blues,
You big stiff, you lucky so-and-so.
No tempo this time, no tonic,
No mode, nothing but a crude rune
As a cue to vamp on your own swan song.

So it goes. It's your wake, so
It's all a cool cat can do now
To go deep, way deep down
Into the pitch-dark of the soul
With no beat, no root, no hook

To bop to, no clefs for your riffs, no
Scaffold of chords, no chart you know
By heart, no ghost of a groove, no
So-la-ti-do, no tapping toe . . . so
Here goes, just you and your ax

Saying so long to what gets you
Only so far on chops and licks
As down you go, tooting your horn
In the cold cold ground till breath do
You part and it's on with the show.

THE GAME OF ROBBERS

I

The pieces can move and take in any direction.
The players take turns at marshaling mayhem.

The Romans called it Ludus Latrunculorum.
Some believe it was stolen from the Egyptians.

On a cartoon papyrus in the British Museum
A billy goat is playing against a lion.

A piece can leapfrog a foe if a cell is open,
But never catapult over one of its own kind.

No one knows when they turned into little men.
The Greeks called them dogs, but the scheme was the same:

Twelve squares by twelve, and on either end
Five rows of six figures, made of wood or bone.

A thinking man's game, most sources contend:
A means of keeping one's wits in fighting trim.

The tokens were soldiers in the original versions.
No one can explain how they came to be villains.

Here's a decimated phalanx from an Etruscan tomb.
Grave robbers made off with the lion's share of them.

In Varro's magnum opus on the native lexicon,
The board doubles as a grid for Latin declensions.

The object is to rub out your opponent's men
One by one, between two desperadoes of your own.

From the diminutive of *latro*: little highwayman.
One man's recreation is another man's revelation.

II

Plato tells us the game was Thoth's invention.
Still another permutation was played by the Assyrians.

Not to be mistaken for Ludus Duodecim Scriptorum:
Not so cutthroat, an early form of backgammon.

Dark plays against light: an obsidian battalion
Taking on a rival clan of ivory or porcelain.

The markers were legions before they were brigands.
Something must have gone missing in the translation.

And here's Queen Hatshepsut's set in mint condition.
All her draughtsmen sport the heads of lions.

The name of the game in Greek means "little stones."
They called the board "the city." No one knows how come.

Some claim the pieces were ranked in stations, like chessmen.
Others say they all played havoc with equal freedom.

From Ovid we learn another cunning stratagem:
Play robbers before bed, and let your flame win.

The lion is handing the little ram's head to him.
You can tell by the big bag of tokens he's taken.

In thieves' cant a constable was called a *myrmidon*.
Any form of armed robbery was known as a *game*.

The hieroglyphs tell us that all the noble ones
In the Kingdom of the Dead play on and on.

No one has played it for nearly a millennium.
De gustibus non est disputandum.

III

What's a mercenary to do when the divisions tramp home?
Some must have turned to lives of petty crime.

According to the don who made it his mission
To reassemble "the bones of the entire skeleton,"

One has to play with ferocious concentration
Lest all be lost in haste or hesitation.

And it says here that anyone who won the scrum
Was called *Dux* or *Imperator*—king of the little men.

The counters were minions before they were ruffians.
One man's diversion is another man's devotion.

When the disguised Athena steals into Odysseus's home,
She finds the suitors killing time with their little stones.

No one knows who wrote the long-winded poem
In praise of Piso the counsel, an adept at the game.

Boards of silver and marble have been found in the ruins:
Baubles fit for an emperor, or a robber baron.

The words "chess" and "check" come to us from the Persian.
The word *Schach* is used for both terms in German,

Which already meant "robbery" in the homeland idiom.
And how do you say chess in Latin? *Ludus latrunculorum*!

If there's honor among thieves, here's your dream team:
The rank and file mustered in armed rows and columns.

Some think the mock combat spawned a Latin maxim:
Ad incitas redigere—"to reduce to desperation."

IV

The hieroglyphs inform us that all the noble ones
In the Kingdom of the Dead play on and on

All afterlife long, and who can blame them?
All that's left for them to conquer now is boredom.

Under Roman law, games of chance were forbidden.
Only contests of skill could be played in the open.

Everyone played: plebeians and patricians,
The smart set, the riffraff, women and children.

The body count mounts as the turf war grinds on.
Is a henchman a hitman by another name?

Don't play harum-scarum. You'll imperil your men.
Don't play possum. You'll pen yourself in.

On a black-figure amphora in the Vatican Museum,
Ajax and Achilles are squaring off in the round,

Their spears on their shoulders as they lock horns.
There's no telling which one has the upper hand.

Piso was top dog. No one could touch him.
Maybe he was a con man. Maybe he gamed the system.

And here's a maven who wants to call it Ludus Praedonum:
"You are literally 'stealing' your opponent's men."

Soldier on, little robbers. Spring into action.
One man's compulsion is another man's conviction.

I'm playing a mug's game with you, my fiends.
History doesn't repeat itself, but sometimes it rhymes.

V

Martial was a fan: "Give me my books and a game
Board with stones, and I'll be happy as a clam."

The counters were troopers before they were hoodlums.
Who can say where battle lines end and badlands begin.

Now there's a simulacrum app you can play online:
"The rules have been imagined based on information found."

Achilles and Ajax can't stop. Some say the scene
Depicts a fabled dogfight from a lost epic poem:

The alpha warriors in full armor on their urn
Have forgotten there's a real campaign going on.

Also lost, alas: the noted Suetonius tome *On Games*,
Our last best hope for rustling up the rules of thumb.

Your move: aim for some Machiavellian equilibrium
Between wanton aggression and wily evasion.

To play well takes work—*quod erat demonstrandum.*
Gamesmanship puts the *tempus fugit* in the *ad infinitum.*

The young Linnaeus, combing Lapland for specimens,
Found something else that captured his imagination:

An old Norse game played on scored reindeer skin
With stones and bones by the last keepers of the flame.

Martial again: "If robber warfare is your game,
Here's your set of soldiers, made out of gems."

One man's ambition is another man's allusion.
To allude means to play. Everyone wins.

VI

Or should we call it a draw? All's a muddle, a midden:
Bits and pieces, odds and ends, a congeries of citations,

Inklings and gleanings from museums and poems,
An omnium-gatherum of antiquarian annotation.

The Pharaohs called it Tau, but here's the conundrum:
Seems for them it was a race game, not a war game.

Aristotle once likened a stateless vagabond
To a game piece off on a square by its lonesome.

Will the lion next match up against a Christian?
One man's subversion is another man's salvation.

Saint Augustine decried the rampant form of imperium
He called the "bandit state," or *grande latrocinium*.

Then there's Seneca's tale of a certain stoic citizen
Who played right up to the brink of his execution

And had one last request for Caligula's centurion:
Let it be known the dead man was ahead by one.

Made out of gems? Maybe for the Equestrians,
But the hoi polloi got by with unprecious stones.

Scratch some lines in the sand and they're sure to come:
Warlords, gangbangers, rogues, thugs, soldiers of fortune.

One man's deception is another man's discretion.
The pieces can move and take in any direction.

Some of this is contention. The rest is quotation.
One man's information is another man's inspiration.

EARTHLY THINGS

Historia universal de las cosas de Nueva España (1577)

What is the name of the plant?
What does it look like?
What does it cure?
How is the medicine made?
How is it taken by the sick?
Where is it found?

What is the name of the animal?
What animals does it resemble?
Where does it live?
Why does it have this name?
What does it look like?
What habits does it have?
How does it feed and hunt?
What sounds does it make?

DEVIL'S ROPE

First the strands of iron drawn out long and fine
Then the things like fangs in the demand for pain

First the newfound land the vast open plain
Then all the things to cast out and pen in

First the one thing and then the other thing
First the pathbreaking then perfecting the thing

First one twining span one twanging harp-string
And then all kinds of painstaking finetuning

First the plain old kind then the newfangled one
First the broken ground then all hell rushing in

And then the cunning twist that seals everything
First the new thing and then the next new thing

First one keen iron talon one patented thorn
Then two thousand versions in the same vein

First the one thing woven round the other thing
Then one long gashing tangle stopping at nothing

Then each sticking point longing to sink into skin
First this one then that one everything closing in

In the beginning a tingling bee-sting of a thing
And in no time an infernal serpentine plaything

First one glinting prick then the demon spawn
And then the one sure thing a thing in pain

First a line in the sand then slinking along
First an inkling of pain then the real thing

And then cloven spurs jabbing in every direction
And then the unveiling of the bristling accordion

And then no-man's-land on the horizon
And then the perfection of concentration

And by then the bane of any earthbound thing
First one damn thing then another damn thing

And no end to honing the fine line between
No end of pain and someone saying when

MADHOUSE PROMENADE

One more time, boys, round the bark, the bark
Locked fast in an endlessness of ice, the ice
Still on the march where open sea should be, the sea
We last saw laid to rest beneath the ice, the ice
We're sick of trekking on, so once more round the bark.

One and all now, round the deck, our beaten track
Through thick and thin in times like these that rack
Seamen's souls, stopped cold in our dicey race
To be there first, fetched up so far from anyplace close
It's anyone's guess if we're adrift or aground.

Time to work the kinks out, buckos, round and round
The half-cracked deck like a lark on the boardwalk
Back in the day, and this time let's pick up the pace
With a skip in your step, your ship doc's new trick
To bring the spirits of our skeleton crew around.

One by one, then arm and arm, the best advice
For the shell shock in the unmapped polar wake
When you're in too deep and any mind's bound
To come unwound, a brisk jaunt through the murk
For its own bracing sake, roundabout in a trice.

One step, two step, round and round, the wreck
Our rock, our walkabout, the route that must suffice
When it's dusk round the clock on the unseen sea, the sea
Drowned out in the bedlam trample of ice, the pack ice
Keeping us in our place, trooping round and round the bark.

TO THE BEATERS

No way to see you whole. That means you've done good work.
You didn't leave your mark, and that shows you know your stuff.
You're there and not there. You're up to your old tricks.

Not a living or a calling, but you must have had your adepts:
Some who boned up on the fly, those with a native gift.
There and not there, your whereabouts still in dispute.

Partridge, sage grouse, moorhen; woodcock, rock dove, snipe;
The king stag and royal boar, the last great herd of aurochs—
You roused and you drove them, dragooned for the nonce.

No manuals, no primers, no schools, no guilds, no troupes.
You've got no future, but you've handed down your trade secrets:
Quick-thinking feet, a foxy streak, a crack sixth sense.

What trusty implements, if any? A good stout stick?
Something tinny to bang on, a rag to flap like wingbeats?
No way to know for sure. You're covering your tracks.

There and not there—we're playing blindman's buff.
No way to flesh you out, no picking up your scent.
You're giving us the slip. You're skulking in plain sight.

Let no past master disparage your body of work.
Ask the hart and the hind, the vixen and the mink.
You flushed them into the wold to meet their fate.

Where is the boundary between a task and a craft?
Someone gave the high sign. Somehow you sorted out
An ad hoc system of commands, a makeshift script:

When to fan out and when to smartly close ranks,
When to hang back and when to pick up your step,
Angle downwind as one and commence the chase

By sealing off the brake and slashing through the copse.
Lords and viceroys, rajas and emirs, sultans and khans,
Sovereigns in skins and furs, barons armed with hawks—

You harried their quarry, you hastened their bloodbaths,
There and not there, noises off, a masque in the rough.
The fine rout was your art. No way you were hacks:

Ask the bear and the pard, the bengal and the roebuck.
You shadowed their spoor, you harrowed their haunts,
You swiped a march on the wolf pack, and the jig was up.

The Worshipful Company of Beaters? That's a joke:
You were flunkies and lackeys, dogsbodies and grunts,
Scarcely a cut above the poor doomed brutes.

There and not there—we're scrabbling in the dark.
No way to see you whole, no telling your prints apart.
You're anywhere you are. You're forever in pursuit.

BREAKER BOY

He's got his boy to carry round
Wherever he goes. He's gone down
To the mines too many times.
Wherever he goes, he's got his boy
To carry round.

He's nine, he's ten,
He's a little old man. He knows
What the other boys are saying:
He's got his boy to carry round
Wherever he goes.

He's a breaker boy. He's got
One job. He straddles the chute
On his bit of plank planted
Atop the slant, pawing out slate
As the slag rumbles down.

He's got his boy to carry round
Wherever he goes. That's what they say
Whenever a boy goes round
In the shoulders, bent over his task
Ten straight hours a day.

He's nine, he's ten, he's been
Around. He's got that look you get
When you live half your life
In the breaker shaft, shift
After shift astride your trough.

Wherever he goes, he's got his boy
To carry round. Wherever he goes,
There he is, his boy in tow,
The boy he's got to carry round
Wherever he goes.

He's no schoolboy. He knows
What he knows. He's got
His one little step. He's got
The squat down. He looks like
He's about to pray,

Pray to the deep dark
Hole in the ground. He's got
That look: black with soot,
Half-cracked, hell-bent, a boy
Who's got to carry the day.

He's a breaker boy. He's got
What it takes, six days a week.
He's got that gait you get
When you've gone round the bend,
Lugging your boy along.

His boy, his boy, wherever
He goes. Wherever there's coal,
There's coal to be broken down.
Wherever there's a breaker, that's
Where his boy can be found.

He's been around. Nothing gets
By him. He's got one good eye,
That boy. He's got the knack
For snatching chunks he knows
Won't burn, carrying on

In the long line of boys
Who man the mines. He's got
The drill down cold. He knows
One slip can take a finger off
Or maybe bury a boy.

Wherever he goes, he's got his boy
To carry round: high and low,
All around town, away in the meadows
Beyond the bare motherlode
Where no other boy goes.

He's a breaker boy. Today's the day
A newspaperman is scratching down
What they say they say when it shows.
He's got his boy to carry round
Wherever he goes.

FEAT

Prowess is never so redoubtable
As when known to progress by
Imperceptible degrees, little by
Little until the most remarkable
Deed becomes the demonstrable
By-product of some humble
Routine, a process so intangible
As to resemble an invisible
Bulwark against the most formidable
Mortal trial, the same principle by
Which days are said to crawl by
And yet fly—as when a little boy
Ambling by the family stable
Hefts a calf's bony wobble
Without a lick of trouble
And proceeds to test his mettle by
Making it his indefatigable
Daily constitutional, until by
And by he's the veritable
Stuff of fable, that invincible
Classical grappler hailed by
His people as impossible
To topple from his pedestal, thereby
Lending a little less inconceivable
Or a thimbleful more irresistible
Weight to those who swear by
How he keeps in fighting trim by
Toting on his back a bull.

SILK QUARTER CHORUS

Ours are the saris no sunset can touch.
Ours the finespun stuff that fills a room with surf.
We root in the dust. That's us underfoot.

Here all the reeling is still done by hand.
The smaller the fingers, the finer the feel.
That sheen is a must. That's where we come in.

Ours the fuming vats, the reeking swill
That cooks the cocoons until they come free.
It's up to us to skim them off in time—

One by one, each one an unwound strand
That goes on and on, a wonder to behold.
It was the worm's secret, and now it's ours.

We unwind and unwind and when we're done,
The filaments must be rewound into the skeins
Renowned as "woven water" from our looms alone.

The uproar, that's ours: a river of raw yarn
Running through our days, rattling our bones.
On it goes. We get a grub's-eye view:

The streaming fibers crisscross rapid-fire,
The bobbins whip up the gossamer luster,
The spindles whirl away in blurs of hues.

That's us huddled for hours, hooked at the hip.
The weavers wield the warp. The weft is ours.
It's up to us to keep the whole swath taut

To make sure the shimmer never wavers
And every hairsbreadth caresses like the next.
Sometimes we screw up. You can tell by our welts.

Ours the whispering veils, the blazing shrouds,
The thrashing saffron of the throngs on the ghats.
Some of us were bonded in the womb—

Born yesterday, and already old hands.
We work off the debt, but the books are cooked.
A tattered moth told us, giving up the ghost.

We have no letters. Feed us these lines.
That's our stitch in your side as you ply our wares.
It was our little secret, and now it's yours.

NIGHT OF THE LIVING HOUSES

Little Nemo in Slumberland (1909)

You asked her would she care if you asked to see her home
She said no she wouldn't care if you asked to see her home

Then the little mixer was over and it was time for all you young ones
To say your good-byes to everyone and begin to find your way home

Out you went *goodnight goodnight* and there you were in the empty street
The two of you in your natty hats and coats hoofing past rowhouse
                                           after rowhouse

The big full moon was the golden of her hair ballooning sudden there
O good golly half a fingertip above the rooftop of that last flophouse

She asked you aren't you afraid to walk all the way back in the dark
You told her no m'am naw not me I like it fine I feel right at home

But it was late late later than you thought not another living soul in sight
Just here and there a brushstroke of lamplight inside some night owl's house

Side by side two inky forms inching down the yawning avenue then coming
                                          to a bend
And still no end to the mountains of brownstones the canyon of rooms
                                        so far from home

She said to you look look what is that and you said I see it too huh
One stoop up on its haunches and just like that a long-legged house

The macadam glazed in amber now the moon a fireball the gleaming Gotham
                                       of your dreams
A funhouse a madhouse a haunted hothouse no place you could ever call home

You said let's cross here to be safe herding her over the street's bright crease
When oh no look another one lurching to its feet a knock-kneed hulk
                                                                              of a house

And then holy moly the whole moonstruck block the next panel over rearing up
                                                                on giant bullfrog shanks
A chain gang a conga line *run run* the windows blazing but nobody home

She bleated in her last little bubble *save me save me* where are you see see
                                                                here they come
You blubbered here I am run but splat you're underfoot look out a house
                                                                on the loose a house

O boyo you little nobody your nightshirt in knots back to bed now me too
                                                                never at home
Even in my own house my own room my own skin sweet skin never at home

LITTLE BOOK OF TRADES

There is a plate to each trade.

Look here, little one:
There was a yesteryear
When you might have been
A tanner of leather,
A dresser of timber,
A cooper or mason
By penchant or station,
A little go-getter,
Bright as a button.

Here's where you'd begin
To form your keen plan,
Or so it says here:
Running your finger
Over each deft figure
The printer handpicked for
This cunning edition
Expressly for children,
Looking into your future.

Look, here's the currier,
The dyer, the potter,
The burly soap-boiler,
The dapper waterman,
All bound up together:
See how the engraver
Looks over the shoulder
Of each one in action
For your instruction.

Here was your primer
On what a vocation
Called for back then
For you to pore over
From cover to cover:
The smith's iron hammer
Hammering on iron
Its own little lesson
In spirit and letter.

Don't look for your father,
My little swing-man:
There's no woolgatherer,
No hairsplitter here,
Though were I a time-traveler
This last one's the one
I'd hanker to master
As the pursuit to pass on
To my only son—

Look, it's the typefounder
With his gauges and gravers,
Turning out new letters one
By one with precision
In profusion, all in a lather
If for no other reason
Than one more job well done
Makes you a little better maker
For your near and dear.

REFRAIN

Big house little house back house barn
A farmhouse a homestead a little song

Form and function one and the same
One roofline one compound home sweet dung

Downhome vernacular rambling on
Going in one ear and out the other end

Sing it from the rooftops style is the man
Big house little house back house barn

A room is a frame is a scheme is a charm
Bless the hardscrabble we hunker down on

Round and around crack of noon stroke of dawn
An old children's playtune a homespun sound

One by one going going going gone
Big house little house back house barn

THREE RIDDLES FROM THE WORD HOARD

Exeter Book No. 24

I'm a creature to conjure with, a chorus by myself.
I can bay like a bloodhound, bleat like a billy goat.
I can do the goose honk and the hawk shriek.
Here's how I keen in the key of the kite,
Here's an earful of the eagle's war cry.
Now I'm a gyrfalcon, now I'm a gull—
A mime in my prime, making my name.
I've got a G, I've got an I,
An A and an E, an M and a P.
See what it spells and say who I am.

Exeter Book No. 15

My throat's a torch   the rest of me rust
From head to haunch   I hotfoot it off
Ready to rumble   That's my ruddy pelt
Bristling in streaks   Those spikes and sparks
Are my ears and eyes   I steal on my toes
Across the green downs   Dark will be the day
If the hellhound comes   harrying here
Where I've gone to ground   with my little ones

The brute's hot breath   at our door
Will doom my brood   to a bloody end
Unless I call on all   my canny wiles
And seize on a scheme   to save our skins

If he bulls into   our burrow hideout
On his belly   baying for our bones
It would be folly   to fight him there
So panting panting   I'll forge a path
Headlong through   our cloud-high hillside

Here's how a mother   must make haste
To hustle her children   away from harm
Spirit us up up out   by a secret route
In the pitch-black peat   like a thing possessed

If the punk still wants   a piece of me
Bring it on   I'll double back
All ablaze inside   bolder than before
And terrible will be   the turf battle
On the hillcrest   under the earth candle
When I turn this time   with tooth and nail
On the unleashed fiend   I'll fly from no longer

Exeter Book No. 85

My home harps on as I hold my tongue—
The maker has matched us, so we must
Stick together. I'm the swifter,
Sometimes stronger; he outlasts me.
Whenever I rest, he rolls right along.
I'll dwell in his din for all my days:
If I go it alone, I'm a ghost.

BARBARIAN

Three hundred lashes for the waters three hundred strokes for the waves
The straits the whitecaps the riptides the pitching swells the crushing depths

Three hundred lashes for the wicked current the insolent brine
      the taunting chop
Three hundred blows for the body of water that dares to bar the way

Clattering fetters for the whirlpools clanking shackles for the waterspouts
Branding irons for the rank salt the rogue surf the upstart spume and froth

For disdain this flagrant for devastation so wanton bring on the beaters
The branders the brandishers of chains the bullyboys the breakers of wills

After the cables snap the winches shatter the heads roll the span goes under
Before the new master builders the better makers begin from scratch

Let there be whiplash after whiplash after whiplash thrashing upon thrashing
Let there be the howling of curses the everlasting scourges of words

For such rampant scorn for great things in store there can be no reprieve no
      sparing the rod
The bullwhip the billy club the blowtorch the double manacle the iron hand

After wading out of the boiling wake before pawing over the wrack and ruin
Call out the floggers the flayers the bloody ballbusters the merchants of pain

Let the waves know what wrath is what spite is how much it burns and stings
What it means to be thwarted shafted smited stricken beyond reckoning

And then keep the whip strokes coming make them rain down on the hot sands
The stones the shells the shingle the cobble the alien shoreline the false horizon

And on all things up and down this spine of land that love to goad the wave on
The four winds the thunderheads the falls far off the creaming rapids bent on
      ravishing the reefs

And on anything shiny scaly slimy showy shadowy that sore offends the soul
In its throes the gnashing shoals the swarms of wings the hardcore scavengers
      of flesh and bone

And with each searing lash each racking wrist-snap make it count cry it out let
      it be known
There can be no turning back no letting up no choking back the bitter words
      that salt the wound

Let the savage waters suffer ever after let each horsewhipped comber hear
      as never before
What a seething thing a tongue is what a torment is to come when what
      is said is meant

MURDER BALLAD

Hey nonny nonny, anybody, lend me your ears.
This one is sure to play chimes down your spine.
Yonder by the river come stepping two sisters.
The older one pushes the younger one in.

Don't ask why, laddie: fa la la, tum ti tum.
Anon wrote the thing and I'm robbing her blind.
Sister O sister, pray give me your hand—
But when the stave ends she's already gone.

Wellaway, so la me: there she goes, way downstream.
She's a slip of a thing, and the current is strong.
Sometimes she sinks and sometimes she swims.
There should be a catch in the throat when it's sung.

The miller's son first thinks he spies a swan
Down down where green grow the rushes-o.
Da, Da, Da, can you see? Shut down the dam—
It's a lass all in white in the millrace below.

Now they fish her out and lay her body down,
Crying O my O the dreadful wind and rain.
There's gold on her fingers and silver in her hair
And this time around they go and strip her bare.

Hit a chord, homey? Fie lay diddle lie day.
Two lines on and already she's picked clean.
Then one spring day a songcatcher chances by
With a hy downe derrie downe bonny doon.

So he gets down to work, badda-bing bada-boom,
And he makes him a fiddle from her pretty breastbone,
And he makes fiddle pegs from her fine finger bones,
And he makes fiddle strings from her long honey mane.

Sometimes she sighs when he plucks a string.
Sometimes the damning name trips off her tongue.
Sometimes she cries O the wind and the rain.
If it's the same every time, you're singing it wrong.

That's all she wrote, baby. There, there. Hear, hear.
Blood under the bridge, news that stays news.
One sister was dark and the other was fair
And one sang a song called "The Green-Eyed Blues."

There it goes again: that killer refrain,
With a wah-wah wonder, da-do run-run.
Who knows why some stuff gets under your skin?
Hey nonny nonny, and the beat goes on.

SAYING

Smart as a whip? How smart
    is that? Smart enough to prick
up ears at a snap? Smart

enough to know what's sport
    and what's not? Smart enough not
to leave a mark yet make

your point felt? Smarter
    than the belt that smote
your own smart ass? Smarter

than the sharpest tool in the shed
    you were told not to touch? Too
smart to try to act as if

you can wipe the blank slate
    to outstrip what still hurts? Too
smart to be smitten

by the thought that you'll
    learn to hit on her or her yet,
after all that hard work

to master your stroke? Far too
    smart to toil for squat, far
smarter than any artful dodger

who ever beat the rap, such
    a smarty-pants savant you can
make a steel trap weep, talk

smack to the stacked deck, bust
    the chops of bad luck, stick it
to the smart set, no sweat? So

smart as to think you can sort
    out black and white brute
fact by brute fact, the dark

back scored with bright stripes
    in the stunned tintype? As
smart as it takes to crack

the code, to hack the site,
    to beat the street, to bet
your life on how to lick

the gene gone rogue? Smarter
    by half than the smart
bomb the smart phone set

off in the market quarter,
    whipping the scapegoats
into smoking bits? Wicked

smart, smart as it gets,
    way too smart to lash out
to spite your own pelt

when you've spit the bit,
    even when it smarts
like a bitch? As smart as

all that, so bloody brilliant
    you can scare up the wit
to whip an old saw

into shape? Smart enough not
    to beat the dumb beast
that's bitten the dust? Smart

enough to be taught new
    tricks, you battered mutt? Smart
enough to grasp what's at stake

when you can't speak straight? Smart
    enough to know how to start
over and when to stop?

SUNSHOWER

Down South, you say the devil is beating his wife.

In Hindi and Sinhalese: the fox's wedding.

Orphan's tears, in Lithuanian; in Arabic, the rats are getting married.

In the Philippines, a *tikbalang*'s wedding: the demon horse taking him a mate.

In Finnish, a wedding in hell; in Polish, the witches are making butter.

Sun shining, rain falling: quick, what do you say?

In Zulu, monkey's wedding; in Afrikaans, jackal is marrying wolf's wife.

In Rio, snail's wedding day: all slick and silvery, a slither of rainbow
above the favelas.

Ghost rain, in Hawaiian; in Armenian, the wolf is giving birth
on the mountain.

Bright sun, hard rain: the devil's at it again, whaling away on his
trouble and strife.

A funfair in hell, if you speak Dutch; in Tamil, fox and raven getting hitched.

In Catalan, a little saying: it rains, it shines, the witches comb their hair.

In Cajun Country, you can go further: the devil is beating his wife and
marrying his daughter.

Sun-drenched, soaked through, squinting, dripping: speak now or forever
bite your tongue.

Naked rain, in Gujarati; on the floodplains of the Punjab, the one-eyed jackal's lucky day.

In Galician, an impish variation: the devil is beating the women with knives and spoons.

In Dakar, someone hears a cabbie say, "Rain and sun, hyena's baby about to die."

Sunny, rainy, wicked cool, passing strange: a touch of water witchery, a whiff of sulfur.

Devil's wedding, in Bengali; in Bulgarian, bear's kissing his new bride.

In Portuguese, you get to choose: rain and sun, snail's wedding; sun and rain, widow's marrying again.

In Kurosawa's *Dreams*, a scene called "Sunlight through the Rain"—a wedding party of fox spirits in slow drumbeat procession through the woods, spied on by a boy.

Sun's out, but the wind shifts, and now it's coming down: you're hot, you're wet, you can't say when you last saw the wolves and tigers taking vows.

Dearly bedeviled, we are gobsmacked here today in this pelting sunshine, this blazing downpour—

Do you take this hellrake, this wild child, this monkey's uncle, this demon lover, this foxy sweet-talker, in heatstroke and in cloudburst till inferno or derecho do you part?

Printer's devil, this one's for you: somewhere, somehow, sunlit rainfall for a spell, and someone looking up and saying what anyone in these parts might say.

OAK APPLE

If there's a worm, a year
To prosper. If a spider,
Woes without number.
If a fly, all will be fair.
If a core ajar, beware.

Year of the worm, you're
In clover. Fly in there, you're
In the clear. An eye for
An eye, murmurs the spider.
Neither hide nor hair, no cure.

Another year, another
Hoard to gather. O Sister
Wasp, what lot's in store?
Your cradle's our ledger.
Our knock's at your door.

Crack one open if you dare.
One thing ripens, the other
Festers. Here's your future
Lurking in its amber sphere,
Sweet or bitter, foul or fair.

If a worm this year, hunger
No more. If a fly, sing for
Your supper. If a spider,
Caterwaul you a river.
If no answer, say a prayer.

O'O

Below each wing, a regal glow,
Oh so opulent as away you flew.
Who could help but ooh and aah?

A jackdaw's bill, a build like a crow.
Black as coal but for those precious few
Tufts of gold, your fatal flaw.

Just for show—hubba-hubba, oo-la-la!—
But even so, pretty touch and go
When every soul wants a piece of you.

The potentates of your archipelago
Knew how to imbue all with awe:
No less a lustrous hue would do

Than you and you and you and you,
Woof by golden woof to halo
A torso in all your sovereign aura.

How now, gewgaw? Here's a clue:
The ghostly echo of your aloha
Rhymes with zero, ringing hollow.

So much for you. You told us so.
Oh-oh, oh no: too good to be true.
Now your name is writ in lava.

Too bad it wasn't decreed taboo
To vamoose with your gilt insignia,
Or anyhow, a big no-no.

You told us so. Cue your tremolo.
Here but for us gone gaga go you.
Sayonara, que sera sera:

Your no-show is the new incognito
À la the dodo and the moa
In a who's who of bugaboo and rue.

Here's a shot of you in full regalia:
Too too solid in chiaroscuro,
Your toe tag scrawled like an IOU.

O o'o, woe is you: no voodoo
Can woo you back for a last hurrah.
So much for you. You told us so.

XYLOTHEQUE

Look it up: each piece of work
In its rightful place, each bookcase
Chockablock with codexes
Of every type, lest we forget
To know of what we speak.

All well and good to hew
To the spirit of the letter, but here
Let the bookworm behold each opus
In its element, the better to grasp
The true grain of the thing.

Pick one out: that's the heft
A wordsmith covets, the stuff
Blockbusters are made of, a text
That's a handbook on itself
Right here at your fingertips.

Lest we forget: each book a block
Unlike the next, a complete set
To leaf through when all but
The artifact is lost, each work
The last word on its subject.

Or better yet, each book a box
For taking stock, the contents
Spelled out with a strip of bark
Along the spine, a work of art
Made out of what it's all about.

PARADISE

Mandeville's Travels

What can I say? I've never been there. I can only tell you what I've heard.

You can't get there from here. You can't get there by land. There are no roads.

There are cliffs and rocks no man can cross, wastes full of wild beasts
   and untold haunts.

You can't get there by water either. The rivers run too far, too fast, headlong
   for the falls.

All around you there's roaring, waves smashing. No man can hear another man
   cry out.

Many are known to set off in search of a passage, but nobody yet has found
   the way.

There are no maps or charts. There are no landmarks. You can't steer
   by the stars.

Many try. They all fail. Upstream, downstream, true north, due west—
   no one comes close.

Some turn to stone by sundown, done in by the strain, never heard from again.

Some abandon all hope and go under, no match for the rips, the deeps, the
   pouring rush.

Some return home, but can no longer see. Some come back, but can't
   hear a thing.

You can't get there from here. It is far beyond. Something always goes wrong.

No man finds his way there without his maker's say-so, from everything I hear.

There's nothing more I can tell you. That's all I've heard. I've never been there.

NIGHTINGALE FLOOR

In the innermost room
Within the inner sanctum
Of nesting planes and turns,
An ingenious means
Of making enemies known:

In each hewn inch, in between
Each unseen seam in the grain
Where nails were driven home,
A nightingale singing in
Piercing strains, slipping in

And out of tune each time
A step is taken that can
Be mistaken for meaning harm,
And then a thousand and one
Of its kind joining in . . .

Or instead you can begin
To turn your own thin skin
Inside out until you're the one
On the outside looking in
As you sound the alarm—

No asylum but the one known
To a lone sparrow blown in then
Out of a banquet hall from gloom
To gloom in a vision, that one
Bright instant in between.

LITTLE NARROWS

No lie, look here—so
Little, so narrow, it's got
No middle, a matchstick inlet,
A little shuttle to get
Across it, so long, hello.

Make that so little, so
Narrow, bet your shadow
Beats us to it, better not
Fidget or you'll miss it, no
Kidding, kiddo.

Narrows, not shallows—no
Little bridge over it, no
Long way around it, so
Here's the two-bit ferryboat
About to spirit us straight

Into the narrow channel no
Bigger than a moat or wallow
With its piddling cargo of fellow
Small-fry carfuls, the far shore so
Nearby you could spit on it.

So long, land ho, don't forget
To write—so little, so
Narrow, no wonder it's cut
Out for us, the closest we'll get
To a perfect fit.

CORN MAZE

Here is where
You can get nowhere
Faster than ever
As you go under
Deeper and deeper

In the fertile smother
Of another acre
Like any other
You can't peer over
And then another

And everywhere
You veer or hare
There you are
Farther and farther
Afield than before

But on you blunder
In the verdant meander
As if the answer
To looking for cover
Were to bewilder

Your inner minotaur
And near and far were
Neither here nor there
And where you are
Is where you were

LACRIMARIUM

Were there a tear
To spare, where better
To be sure the gesture
Would linger than here
In its own little bottle
Blown from a hot bubble
To mirror a tear.

And were there more
Than one could bear,
So much the better
In the hereafter for
The begetter, a little
Vessel to stopper
Sorrow beyond measure.

And were there a tear
Too few, far better to hire
A weeper, for where
But in a tearful little
Jigger does it figure
No one need settle for
Less than a fair share.

Praxitelean
Praxiteles (fl. 375–340 B.C.E.), Athenian sculptor renowned for his marble nudes of the gods, following his own system of proportions for representing the human body. An epigram from *The Greek Anthology* traditionally attributed to Plato attests to the stature of the Praxitelean aesthetic in the classical world: "When Aphrodite saw *Aphrodite of Knidos*, she cried, 'Where did Praxiteles see me naked?' "

Franklin Arithmetic
Adapted, with liberties, from the first edition of *The Franklin Intellectual Arithmetic* (1832), compiled by "E. Davis, A. M., Principal of Westfield Academy."

Of Fast or Loose
Reginald Scot's *The Discoverie of Witchcraft*, first published in London in 1584, is possibly the earliest influential work of its kind, a copious treatise aimed at debunking the existence of "Witches, Divels, Spirits, or Familiars." Billed in later editions as "very necessary to be known for the undeceiving of Judges, Justices and Juries," Scot's exposé on miracles and magic of all stripes included extensive blow-by-blow explanations of common magician's tricks as evidence that the whole of "demonologie" was likewise a sham. The poem's title refers to Scot's description of the rope-conjuring trick that gave rise to the common expression "play fast and loose" (Dover, 1972), 190–91.

Trickeration
The jive dance song "Trickeration" was recorded by Cab Calloway and His Orchestra in New York in October 1931, the same year Calloway's band was hired by the Cotton Club as a replacement for the touring Duke Ellington Orchestra. In short order, the Calloway and Ellington ensembles were installed as the club's two house bands. The poem draws on both the lyrics of "Trickeration" and Calloway's 1938 book *Hepster's Dictionary: The Language of Jive*.

The Magic Moving Picture Book
Unabridged reissue of the London 1898 edition, originally titled *The Motograph Moving Picture Book* (Dover, 1975).

The Study of Butterflies

The English naturalist and explorer Henry Walter Bates first traveled to the Amazon rain forest in 1848, in the company of his friend Alfred Russel Wallace. He remained there for the next eleven years. By the time he returned to England in 1859, he had amassed a collection of more than fourteen thousand species of insects, more than half of them new to taxonomy. Butterflies were a particular passion. Based on his fieldwork on Amazonian butterflies, Bates formulated the theory of mimicry (now known as Batesian mimicry), which he judged to be "a most beautiful proof of natural selection." Charles Darwin, for one, agreed. The passage referenced here comes from chapter 12, "Animals of the Neighborhood of Ega," in the reprint edition of *The Naturalist on the River Amazons* (Dover, 1976), 347–48.

On a Shaker Admonition

"The so-called Millennial Laws of the Shakers, never printed nor even widely circulated in written form, implemented the doctrines of the order, and thus, in effect, greatly illuminate not only its government but the intimate habits and customs of the people." Edward Deming Andrews, *The People Called Shakers* (Dover, 1953), 243. The epigraph is found in part 3, "Concerning Temporal Economy, Section V: Orders Concerning Locks and Keys," 283.

Sand Man

Andrew Clemens (ca. 1857–94) was the premier "sand artist" of his day and, by most estimates, the sole practitioner of his self-taught technique of fashioning elaborately designed sand bottles. Deaf and unable to speak from a young age, Clemens produced most of his work in his hometown of McGregor, Iowa, close to the Pictured Rocks region famous for its variegated sandbanks colored by limestone iron oxide. He is thought to have crafted hundreds of decorative sand bottles for the souvenir trade and on commission, often using up to forty different colors of sand to execute his most intricate scenes and motifs. Only a few dozen survive. For a brief time, he appeared as a sideshow attraction in a Chicago dime museum, where a barker would shatter each sand bottle as soon as it was finished to certify that Clemens's painstaking artistry was the real thing. See Francine Kirsch, "The Sand Man: The Spectacular Sand Bottles of Andrew Clemens," *Antique Trader*, February 25, 2008, and Marian C. Rischmueller, "McGregor Sand Artist," *The Palimpsest* 26 (May 1945): 129–47.

The Rubaiyat of Omar Aqta

"This page probably comes from a gigantic Qur'an that the calligrapher 'Umar Aqta' wrote for the ruler Timur (Tamerlane, d. 1405). Apparently Timur was unimpressed after 'Umar Aqta' wrote a Qur'an so small that it could fit under a signet ring, so the calligrapher wrote another Qur'an so large it had to be brought to Timur on a cart." *Folio from the "Qur'an of 'Umar Aqta',"* ink, opaque watercolor, and gold on paper, Metropolitan Museum of Art.

Painter's Wife's Island

"To which purpose I remember a pretty jest of Don Pedro de Sarmiento, a worthy gentleman who had been employed by his King in planting a colony upon the Streights of Magellan; for when I asked him, being then my prisoner, some question about an island in those Streights, which methought might have done benefit or displeasure to his enterprise, he told me merrily that it was to be called 'Painter's Wife's Island,' saying that whilst the fellow drew that map, his wife, sitting by, desired him to put in one country for her that she, in imagination, might have an island of her own." Sir Walter Raleigh, *The History of the World in Five Books*, bk. 2, chap. 23 (1614).

Song of Nothing

The dozen or so poems written in Occitan by Guilhem IX, duke of Aquitaine (ca. 1070–1127), were the earliest in the language to survive, earning him the sobriquet "the first of the troubadours." This adaptation of *Farai un vers de dreit rein* owes a debt to the English translation and accompanying historical gloss found in W. S. Merwin's *The Mays of Ventadorn* (National Geographic Directions, 2002).

Hanetsuki

Young Woman with Battledore and Shuttlecock (Hanetsuki), Utagawa Toyokuni I (1769–1825), ukiyo-e, Edo period, Museum of Fine Arts, Boston.

Kabocha-Toli

The title is the Choctaw name (literally, "stickball") for the sport now called lacrosse. In his travels through Indian Territory in the 1830s, George Catlin recorded rare eyewitness accounts of full-scale matches in his sketchbooks and journals, scenes he described as "a school for the painter or sculptor, equal to any of those which ever inspired the hand of the artist in the Olympian games or the Roman forum." George Catlin, *North American Indians*, ed. Peter Mat-thiessen (Penguin Books, 1989), 397. Two Catlin oils in particular capture the spectacle of the fray: the portrait *Tul-lock-chish-ko, Drinks the Juice of the Stone, in Ball-Player's Dress* (page 400) and the panoramic *Ball-play of the Choctaw—Ball Up* (page 402). Both these images can be viewed on the website of the Smithsonian American Art Museum (https://americanart.si.edu/artwork/tul-lock-chish-ko-drinks-juice-stone-ball-players-dress-4035) and (https://america-nart.si.edu/artwork/ball-play-choctaw-ball-3885).

Foley Room

Foley art, the reproduction of ambient sounds in postproduction filmmaking, takes its name from its prime innovator, Jack Donovan Foley (1891–1967). Pressed into service with the sound crew converting the Universal Studios silent version of *Show Boat* into the 1929 musical, Foley went on to pioneer many of the techniques for re-creating everyday movie sound effects still in practice today. Synching up convincing footsteps on all kinds of surfaces called for in the scripts was a signature specialty. Foley studios equipped with Foley floors where Foley artists ply their trade continue to play an indispensable role in movie making. As Irish Foley artist Caoimhe Doyle has said, Foley per-formed in faithful Jack Foley fashion still works best for many sounds, "like the kisses and the punches."

Table

Appropriated, with liberties, from "Table of Clever Tricks," in *Clever and Pleasant Inventions, Part One*, by J. Prevost, trans. Sharon King (1584; repr., Hermetic Press, 1998). The book is often acknowledged as the earliest known manual entirely devoted to the art of conjuring. There is no "Part Two."

Carton Fantastique

Jean-Eugène Robert-Houdin (1805–71) was the foremost stage conjurer of his age and, by common consent, the father of modern theater magic. The young Ehrich Weiss paid the ultimate magician's homage to the master when he ad-opted his own stage name—Houdini. Robert-Houdin's memoirs, *Confidences d'un prestidigitateur* (1859), were originally published in an English translation by Lascelles Wraxall and reissued in 1964 under the title *King of the Conjurers*. "To succeed as a conjurer," he wrote, "three things are essential—first, dexter-ity; second, dexterity; and third, dexterity." "Carton Fantastique" (commonly translated as "Robert-Houdin's Portfolio") was an illusion he was said to perform regularly at his Théâtre Robert-Houdin in Paris.

Indian Rope Trick

Peter Lamont, *The Rise of the Indian Rope Trick: How a Spectacular Hoax Became History* (Thunder's Mouth Press, 2004). Lamont's forensic investigation would appear to be the last word in debunking this legendary stage illusion. Then again, as Teller observed in his 2005 review of the book, "When you're certain you cannot be fooled, you become easy to fool" (*New York Times*, Feb. 13, 2005).

The Lion's Bride

The stage illusion described here was the brainchild of Sigmund Neuberger (1871–1911), a master illusionist and quick-change artist who performed worldwide as the Great Lafayette. It became his signature act and the cause of his demise. In the midst of performing "The Lion's Bride" at the Empire Palace Theatre in Edinburgh on May 9, 1911, a fire broke out in the lighting that rapidly consumed the stage as the packed house fled to safety. The Great Lafayette was one of ten people to perish in the blaze, along with the lion. See Milbourne Christopher, *The Illustrated History of Magic* (New York: Crowell, 1973).

On the Spectacles

The *Liber Spectaculorum* (*Book of Spectacles*) was Martial's first published collection of epigrams, written to celebrate the opening, in the year 80, of the Roman Colosseum by the emperor Titus. The main source for these patchwork versions was Kathleen M. Coleman's *Martial: Liber Spectaculorum* (Oxford University Press, 2006).

Ballyhoo

"Chief Zat Zam, member of the Peoria Magicians' Assembly and the last of the Aztecs, died on January 14th, 1936, at Proctor Hospital, Peoria, Illinois, at the age of eighty-seven. Chief Zat Zam was the originator of knife throwing and a builder of many magic illusions. He performed throughout the world, and had a command performance before King George. Members of the Peoria Magicians' Assembly acted as pallbearers." *The Sphinx: An Independent Magazine for Magicians*, February 1936.

Blue Man Song

The song is made up; the case is a matter of record. As Deborah Blum tells it in her 2010 book *The Poisoner's Handbook*, the longtime "Blue Man" of the Barnum traveling circus checked himself into Bellevue Hospital complaining of severe shortness of breath. His death in January 1924 is noted in the records of the New York City Medical Examiner's office, where the autopsy was performed. Toxicologists confirmed an advanced case of argyria, a condition contracted from excessive deposits of silver in the body organs that was known to stain skin tissues a deep grayish blue. It was believed that the Blue Man's indigo hue came from decades of dosing himself with silver nitrate, but that's not what did him in. The official cause of death was pneumonia. * * *With special thanks to Dr. Eugene Beresin*

Ota Benga

Assembled, with liberties, from headlines appearing in several New York City newspapers during September and October 1906. Background sources: Pamela Newkirk, *Spectacle: The Astonishing Life of Ota Benga* (HarperCollins, 2015); Mitch Keller, "The Scandal at the Zoo," *New York Times*, August 6, 2006; and Geoffrey C. Ward, "The Man in the Zoo," *American Heritage*, October 1992.

Solo

"Mingus was a very inventive kind of musician; he seemed to have a storehouse of innovations to spring on us . . . Once when we were playing one of his tunes, 'Ecclesiastes,' I noticed there were no chords when it came time for my solo. He pointed to a picture of a coffin and told me, 'Play that.' " *The Gentle Giant: The Autobiography of Yusef Lateef*, with Herb Boyd (Morton Books, 2006).

The Game of Robbers

The farrago of sources ransacked for all this "antiquarian annotation" defies orderly reckoning. One nonetheless deserves mention: Edward Falkener, *Games Ancient and Oriental and How to Play Them* (1892; repr., Dover, 1961). The book devotes a lengthy chapter to Ludus Latrunculorum, salted profusely with classical references. Falkener, an English architect and sometime classical archaeologist, improbably remains a quotable authority on board games in antiquity, still worth adducing for his unquenchable enthusiasm if not his unquestionable erudition: "It is wonderful that this game should ever have fallen into desuetude, that it should ever have become so completely forgotten, that the most zealous and learned antiquaries should have failed to restore it to light" (page 38).

Earthly Things
Distilled, with liberties, from book 11 ("Earthly Things") in *Historia universal de las cosas de Nueva España* (*The Universal History of the Things of New Spain*), a twelve-volume illustrated compendium on Aztec life orchestrated and assembled by Franciscan friar Bernardino de Sahagún between 1550 and 1580. See Gerhard Wolf and Joseph Connors, eds., *Colors Between Two Worlds: The Florentine Codex of Bernardino de Sahagún* (Florence: Villa I Tatti and Harvard University Press, 2011).

Madhouse Promenade
The Belgian Antarctic Expedition of the *Belgica* was icebound in frozen coastal waters for much of the year 1898. In his chronicle of the voyage, *Through the First Antarctic Night* (1900), the ship's doctor, Frederick A. Cook, recalled his efforts to combat the physical and psychological trials of a "new human experience in a new, inhuman world of ice." Among the remedies Cook prescribed were daily walks around the ship on the pack ice, an exercise routine the crew took to calling the madhouse promenade.

Breaker Boy
The documentary photographer Lewis Hine's portraits of "breaker boys" at work in the coal mines of eastern Pennsylvania were among the most galvanizing images to emerge from the formation of the National Child Labor Committee in 1907. The reform movement was also spurred by a number of unsparing eyewitness reports in the muckraking press, most notably Stephen Crane's article "In the Depths of a Coal Mine" (1894) and John Spargo's book *The Bitter Cry of Children* (1906). The following passage from Spargo's account warrants special notice here:

> Work in the coal breakers is exceedingly hard and dangerous. Crouched over the chutes, the boys sit hour after hour, picking out the pieces of slate and other refuse from the coal as it rushes past to the washers. From the cramped position they have to assume, most of them become more or less deformed and bent-backed like old men. When a boy has been working for some time and begins to get round-shouldered, his fellows say that "He's got his boy to carry round wherever he goes."

Night of the Living Houses

Winsor McCay's landmark Sunday comic strip ran in the *New York Herald* from 1905 to 1911 and in the *New York American* from 1911 to 1914. Taking up a full broadsheet page of the all-color "funnies," each installment portrayed a phantasmagorical dream in bravura detail capped off in the last panel with the same running gag—young Nemo wide-awake in bed in his rumpled nightshirt. See *Little Nemo in Slumberland: So Many Splendid Sundays!* (vol. 1), ed. Peter Maresca (Sunday Press Books, 2005).

Little Book of Trades

Peter Stockham, ed., *Little Book of Early American Crafts and Trades* (Dover, 1976). Facsimile edition of part 1 of the work published by Jacob Johnson in Whitehall (Philadelphia) and Richmond in 1807 under the title *The Book of Trades, or Library of the Useful Arts*. The 1805 British edition received a glowing review from Mrs. Trimmer's *Guardian of Education*: "We recommend this Book as a valuable acquisition to the Juvenile Library. The Plates are uncommonly good."

Refrain

The refrain echoes and plays changes on the title and thesis of Thomas C. Hubka's 1984 study *Big House, Little House, Back House, Barn: The Connected Farm Buildings of New England* (University Press of New England).

Three Riddles from the Word Hoard

For all their down-market associations with playground brainteasers and knock-knock jokes, riddles still ask to be reckoned with as the "dark sayings" that constitute what Richard Wilbur calls "a poetic form of great age, meaning, and persistent vitality." The Anglo-Saxon heritage of riddle telling and riddle cracking is especially vital in its persistence. What makes these sayings "dark" is the secret identity of the poem's speaker or signifier—the upshot of this oral test of wits was to capture the essence of a thing without naming it. The original texts for these three versions are among the ninety-odd catalogued specimens of *enigmata* in the Exeter Book, the tenth-century monastic codex of poetry that remains the single largest trove of surviving Old English literature. The Exeter Book riddles do not come with an answer key, but there is general agreement that the likeliest solutions are magpie or jay (no. 24), vixen (no. 15), and fish and water (no. 85). Numbering follows the system from *The Word Exchange: Anglo-Saxon in Translation*, edited by Greg Delanty and Michael Matto

(Norton, 2011), where the poems first appeared. Background sources: Michael Alexander, trans., *The Earliest English Poems* (Penguin Books, 1966); Kevin Crossley-Holland, trans., *The Exeter Book Riddles* (Penguin Books, 1979); Richard Wilbur, "The Persistence of Riddles," in *The Catbird's Song: Prose Pieces 1963–1995* (Harcourt Brace, 1997).

Barbarian

"When, therefore, the channel had been bridged successfully, it happened that a great storm arising broke the whole work to pieces, and destroyed all that had been done. So when Xerxes heard of it he was full of wrath, and straightway gave orders that the Hellespont should receive three hundred lashes, and that a pair of fetters should be cast into it. Nay, I have even heard it said that he bade the branders take their irons and therewith brand the Hellespont. It is certain that he commanded those who scourged the waters to utter, as they lashed them, these barbarian and wicked words . . ." Herodotus, *The Histories* (Book VII, chapters 34–35), English translation by George Rawlinson (1910). The ancient Greek word *barbaros*, originally a common epithet for all non-Greek-speaking peoples, was meant to mimic the sound of unintelligible babbling.

O'o

"The intricate ceremonial robes of Hawaiian royalty were made from the brilliant plumage of the royal bird, the o'o (*Moho nobilis*). Thousands of these large, confident birds, a species of Hawaiian honeyeater, had to be trapped to get enough feathers to weave the sacred garments . . . The last Hawaiian o'o ['ō'ō, pronounced 'oh-oh'] was seen in 1934." Rosamond Purcell, *Swift as a Shadow: Extinct and Endangered Animals* (Houghton Mifflin, 1999), plate no. 37.

Xylotheque

"The volumes of the *xylotheque*, the 'wooden library,' are the product of a time when scientific inquiry and poetic sensibility seemed effortlessly and wittily married: the Enlightenment of the eighteenth century . . . In the German culture where modern forestry began, some enthusiast thought to go one better than the botanical volumes that merely illustrated the taxonomy of trees. Instead the books themselves were to be fabricated from their subject matter, so that the volume on *Fagus*, for example, the common European beech, would be bound in the bark of that tree. Its interior would contain samples of beech nuts and seeds; and its pages would literally be its leaves, the folios its *feuilles*." Simon Schama, *Landscape and Memory* (Vintage Books, 1996), 18.

Paradise

Reconstituted, with liberties, from *The Travels of Sir John Mandeville*, trans. C. W. R. D. Moseley (Penguin Books, 1983), and *Mandeville's Travels: The Cotton Version*, trans. P. Hamelius (British Library), https://quod.lib.umich.edu/c/cme/aeh6691/1:7.2?rgn=div2;view=toc/.

Nightingale Floor

"In the Edo period, the nightingale floor was a popular acoustic warning system. The principle was very simple: when someone stepped on the floorboards, the nails holding them in place rubbed against metal clamps mounted on the underside of the boards, raising the alarm by creating a squeaking noise that resembled the chirping of the Japanese nightingale." Liner notes for Jan Jelinek, *Uguisubari*, Acoustic Surveillance Series, 7" vinyl single (Faitiche, 2017).

ACKNOWLEDGMENTS

My thanks to the editors of the following publications, in which these poems first appeared: *Agni*: "The Study of Butterflies"; *The American Scholar*: "The Lion's Bride," "Mamihlapinatapai," "On a Shaker Admonition," "Saying"; *The Atlantic*: "Little Narrows," "Yogi Glosa"; *Ecotone*: "Feat," "Xylotheque"; *The Hopkins Review*: "Blue Man Song," "Kabocha-Toli," "Madhouse Promenade," "Nightingale Floor," "Refrain," "Slow Burn," "Table"; *Kenyon Review*: "Carton Fantastique," "Franklin Arithmetic"; *Memorious*: "Sunshower"; *The New Criterion*: "Oak Apple," "Of Fast or Loose," "Song of Nothing"; *New England Review*: "Indian Rope Trick"; *New Ohio Review*: "The Rubaiyat of Omar Aqta"; *Parnassus*: "Ballyhoo"; *Poetry*: "Aria," "Corn Maze," "Lacrimarium"; *Southwest Review*: "Sherpa Song"; *The Yale Review*: "Hanetsuki."

"Aria" was reprinted in *Literature: An Introduction to Fiction, Poetry, Drama, and Writing*, ed. X. J. Kennedy and Dana Gioia, 14th ed. (Pearson, 2019).

"On a Shaker Admonition" was reprinted in *Best American Poetry 2016* and "Sherpa Song" was reprinted in *Best American Poetry 2017*.

"Three Riddles from the Word Hoard" originally appeared individually in *The Word Exchange: Living Poets Translate Anglo-Saxon Poems*, ed. Greg Delanty and Michael Matto (Norton, 2010).